Choose Peace Now

A Sacred Utterance

Leonard Laskow, M.D.

with

Maddisen K. Krown, Ph.D.

Green Heart Living Press

Choose Peace Now
Copyright © 2022 Leonard Laskow, M.D.

All rights reserved. No part of this book may be used or reproduced by any means, graphic, electronic, or mechanical, including photocopying, recording, taping or by any information storage retrieval system without the written permission of the publisher, except in the case of brief quotations embodied in critical articles and reviews.

ISBN Paperback: 978-1-954493-28-5

Cover Design: Mary Ann Pack and Elizabeth Hill
Graphic Design Support: Milena Buncic

This book is designed to provide information and motivation to our readers. It is sold with the understanding that the publisher is not engaged to render any type of psychological, legal, or any other kind of professional advice. The content is the sole expression and opinion of its author, and not necessarily that of the publisher. No warranties or guarantees are expressed or implied by the publisher's choice to include any of the content in this volume. Neither the publisher nor the individual authors shall be liable for any physical, psychological, emotional, financial, or commercial damages, including, but not limited to, special, incidental, consequential or other damages. Our views and rights are the same: You are responsible for your own choices, actions, and results.

Dedication

This book is dedicated to my daughter, Gabriella, who lights up my heart.

Table of Contents

Foreword	7
Preface	9
Introduction	13
Chapter 1: The Collective Dark Night of the Soul	17
Chapter 2: The Game of Awakening	21
Chapter 3: Portals to Peace	35
Holoenergetic Portals to Peace	38
Grounding, Aligning, Centering,	
and The Field of Light	39
Conscious Heart Focus	41
Conscious Heart Focus (Short Version)	45
Mini Balancing Breath	47
Accessing Head and Heart Space	53
Transpersonal Self Alignment	57
Self Harmonizing Process	63
Chapter 4: The Collective Dawn of the Soul	69
Epilogue - Love is the Way	81
Afterword - Ode to Mind	87
What is Holoenergetic® Healing?	91

Foreword

In the midst of these chaotic times, Dr. Leonard Laskow's book, *Choose Peace Now*, offers the nectar of his teachings to those who have a true thirst for Peace.

Now more than ever, we need the guidance of wise beings like Dr. Laskow, who do not just share conceptual information about *peace*, but who truly ARE the peaceful and awakened PRESENCE they point at. Egoless beings who are what they teach – and who also share practical tools that enable every true seeker to shift from *thinking* to *being*, from *form* to *essence*, from the *many* to the *One*.

Dr. Laskow is a pioneer. The Holoenergetic® practice he has designed to experience the formless nature of our being – the flow of Life itself, beyond words and understanding – is unique. And like all pioneers, his work may not be fully recognized in his lifetime. Yet, every single being who will heal and awaken thanks to Holoenergetic®, will contribute to the emergence of a more conscious, loving, and peaceful world. What a joyful perspective!

Choose Peace Now

Back in 2014, when I attended my first Holoenergetic® seminar with Dr. Laskow in Paris, France, I knew my spiritual quest was being answered, and by the end of that day, it was crystal clear to me that I would be devoting my life to Holoenergetic®.

Now, as a Laskow Holoenergetic® teacher and facilitator, it is my deepest wish to transmit these teachings, with respect and integrity – for the greatest good of All.

My heart is filled with gratitude, joy, and respect for Dr. Laskow and his wife, Sama Schurter Laskow. And I am eternally grateful for their unconditional support and loving presence in my life.

Choose Peace Now is a precious gift, offering a rare and beautiful journey for those of you who are called to awaken their essential nature through Love, Forgiveness, Peace, and Oneness. May you receive this gift with an open heart.

LAURENCE LATOUR
Laskow Holoenergetic® Teacher & Facilitator

Preface

Choose Peace Now has been a guiding light in my life for a long time, and now it is part of my trilogy of books.

My first book, *Healing with Love*, guided us into healing. The second book, *For Giving Love* guided us into forgiving, and now this third book, *Choose Peace Now*, guides us into peace.

This is the peace that comes from oneness, from stillness. In other words, we are really choosing what is ever-present, that which always exists. We can choose this – now.

At first, I thought maybe "choosing" is not the right word, because it implies "will," meaning when you choose something you're using your will. But you're really choosing something that is ever-present. It's like choosing the space in this room, which is ever-present. So, it is choosing the space, not the content in the space, choosing the consciousness that is ever-present, which transcends all content.

Choose Peace Now

In the Introduction, I share how this third book was inspired. About how *Choose Peace Now* spontaneously came through me, as divine grace, when one of my students was writhing in pain from the past, and how it brought him back to peace, to the ever-present now.

Choose Peace Now is a call to Essence. To where there is only stillness, oneness, wholeness.

That is what we call eternity beyond time, infinity beyond space – where oneness takes in everything, and no thing.

That is the gift of this book. It is not about help and it is beyond health. Awareness is not about help. Once we have awareness, in the deepest sense, we're beyond the need for help or healing. Awareness is wholeness, oneness, it is the ultimate resource. As you bring awareness to anything, it resolves that thing back into awareness as a wave dissolves back into the ocean.

We can get attached to the form and content, but at some point, we need to transcend "understanding" the form, because understanding is the grasping of the mind. And this awareness, this stillness, is beyond the mind. So, at some point, we transcend the need to understand. And what is left is "Being." If you can just be, then understanding is subsumed by Being.

Preface

The same is true for peace. There is no need to understand what it is, because it is ever-present, as awareness of awareness or consciousness.

We can ask for that which is ever-present – we can Choose Peace Now.

Perhaps this book can be a gift for humanity – a way to embody and experience this truth while we are still here in form. Uttering *"Choose Peace Now"* can bring us into the ever-present space of stillness, peace, awareness, and ultimately, oneness.

This may also be the highest truth at the moment of conscious death. The last three words uttered on this journey of life, that one consciously speaks before what we call physical death, and awakening to a higher consciousness beyond form. *"Choose Peace Now"* can truly be a call to Essence.

You don't have to be enlightened to be aware of awareness, for this Divine sacred utterance to work, because it addresses that which is already present within you. You just have to utter it, mean it, and be with it.

A sacred utterance – Choose Peace Now.

Leonard Laskow, M.D. January 2022

Introduction

Choose Peace Now

When we focus on space, that's peace. Because where there is nothing, no thing – we can feel stillness, peace.

Why Choose Peace Now?

I was giving a Holoenergetic® seminar called "Awakening Your Healing Heart" in Tiburon, California, in the San Francisco Bay area. As part of this seminar, I facilitate the Holoenergetic® Tracing Process, in which you can go back to an earlier time in your life, sometimes even in your mother's womb, or into a previous life, and bring forth something you experienced at that time that is influencing your present life now.

During this Tracing process in which participants were working together in pairs (or dyads as we call them) in different rooms, I heard someone screaming in one of the rooms. I went into that room and saw one of the participants rolling around on the floor and screaming out, "I'm burning! I'm burning!" while furiously patting different places on his body, as if attempting to put out a fire. As it turned out, during his Tracing, he was recalling a time when he was being crucified and set on fire.

I went immediately over to him, got down on my knees, and said spontaneously and firmly, "Choose Peace Now!" I don't know where these words came from, however, I knew I must say this to him because he was not present. He was totally inside whatever was the past experience. As I said "choose peace now" to him, he was able to focus on those words and follow those directions. Very soon, he was taking deep breaths and relaxing. He said, "Oh wow, I was really burning. It was terrible. But now I know I am fine."

That is how I came to know the power in those three words, "Choose Peace Now" and that this is a portal. "Choose" means you have the will to focus your attention, which is focused awareness, which means you can focus your awareness on whatever you choose now, in the present, and you can focus that awareness on the stillness and space of peace.

"Choose" means you have the will to focus your attention, which is focused awareness, which means you can focus your awareness on whatever you choose now, in the present, and you can focus that awareness on the stillness and space of peace.

Choose Peace Now

Everyone has an intuitive sense of peace, and that "now" is the present moment, right here, right now. It also implies that the moment is whatever is arising in the now, and that is what you focus on. But the real now is the space in which objects arise and subside. Therefore, when you say, "Choose Peace Now," you are saying it in the space of now; not so much in the content of the moment, but in the space of the moment. This is another way of talking about "presence," bringing someone into the present. There are different ways to do that. For example, focusing on your breath can bring you into the present, the now.

And so, why "Choose Peace Now"? Well, in the example of the participant who thought he was on fire, he was acting out from conditioning of the past, and it was very important to bring him back into the present moment and recognize that he had the power to choose what to focus his attention on in the moment. Because ultimately this is the primary choice we all have – what is it that we want to focus our attention on? If we want to focus our attention on peace, then that is what we attract to us. And if we want to focus our attention on peace now, then that part of the attraction is focusing on the space of now. And that space of now is the very peace we are choosing.

Choose Peace Now

This book is designed to take you deeper into the wisdom and the steps for choosing peace now in your own life. It lights the way through the game of awakening into pure awareness and oneness, guiding you into the portals of peace, and how to express your essential, loving nature through your life purpose.

We welcome you on this journey of peace.

Chapter 1

The Collective Dark Night of the Soul

All war is also war with yourself – until you connect with the peace within.

Prelude to Transformation

People are often asking about how to deal with the collective nightmare of war, lack, fear, sickness, and suffering – this dark night of the soul that we seem to be going through. Several answers spring to mind, and one is the famous quote from Mahatma Gandhi, "Be the change you wish to see in the world."

This apparent chaos might just be a prelude to transformation, transformation to a new order, a higher level of human consciousness.

This apparent chaos might just be a prelude to transformation, transformation to a new order; a higher level of consciousness.

Choose Peace Now

For transformation to occur, the old form has to die. It has to change. And ultimately, all form is transcended into the unmanifest realm. The content of consciousness is always changing. When we identify with or become attached to the changing content, we set ourselves up for suffering.

Consciousness is the ever-present, underlying awareness, the unchanging background context. Consciousness is the seer or witness of all content that arises and subsides.

Then what do we focus on? The changing form, or the unchanging essence that we call consciousness, or both? The answer is not either/or but both, since form is embodied essence. Consciousness takes shape as form, just as the waves that take form in the ocean are made of water.

And how do we access and live this? By allowing whatever form arises or subsides to come and go without attachment or resistance. This unconditional acceptance of whatever is in this present moment opens the Portal to Presence, which is one with our essential nature, which is consciousness itself.

In what other ways can we focus on and have access to our essential nature, to consciousness itself? At a time of global and personal change, what can we do to ease the transition to a new paradigm? How can we wake up from the collective nightmare

The Collective Dark Night of the Soul

of war, lack, sickness, suffering, and apparent separation?

The key is to shift our attention (focused consciousness) from content to context, from object to observer, to being the Aware Witness – aware of awareness.

The key is to shift our attention (focused consciousness) from content to context, from object to observer, to being the Aware Witness – aware of awareness.

On the outer or content level, life purpose differs from person to person. On the inner or context level, life purpose is the same for all of us – we remember who we truly are as loving awareness itself, at home in Source.

In my seminar, "Opening to Oneness," we share a number of portals to ever-present consciousness by accessing the Aware Witness or Soul. Soul is the simultaneous awareness of unity and uniqueness, the aware witness, the interface between spiritual essence and personal form, and is felt as the energy of Love.

Remember, apparent chaos might just be a prelude to transformation, transformation to a new order, a higher level of human consciousness, to transcendence of the form.

Choose Peace Now

Years ago, an attorney friend of mine who visited Sri Lanka and the ashram of the famous guru Bawa, shared this personal story with me.

Bawa was sitting on a raised platform, when a disheveled man rushed in from the back door, carrying a knife, and started running toward Bawa, shouting, "I'm going to kill you!"

My friend was preparing to tackle the man, when Bawa opened his collar and pulled it down, exposing his neck, and said, "May the taking of this life bring your soul the peace that it seeks." The man suddenly dropped the knife and fell to his knees sobbing. Bawa said to him, "Go home friend, clean up, and come back." Upon returning, the man became a disciple.

Chapter 2

The Game of Awakening

Enlightenment doesn't mean that you no longer have a body. It means that you know you are not only your body. Regardless of how we frame it, our bodies and our mind structures with all their conditioning, are prisms that will always refract the pure light of awareness into the rainbow hues that are uniquely you. The forms are many –
The essence is One.

Awakening to Pure Awareness and Oneness

In my book, *For Giving Love: Awakening Your Essential Nature Through Love and Forgiveness,* I introduce "The Game of Awakening," which models our cyclical journey of awakening from and to Pure Awareness and Oneness.

There is the classic story of the Brahman priest asking Buddha if he was a divine being – a god or demi-god – and Buddha's response was, "I am awakened."

Awakened to what?

The traditions would suggest Buddha – and others who have experienced a deep and profound epiphany of life beyond this veil – were awakened to the illusory nature of what we call reality, recognizing that we are not just our physical bodies, our thoughts, beliefs, sensations, emotions, and the material conditions and "stuff" that manifest in our lives.

Buddha awakened to recognize both the form and the formless as the One.

You may be thinking, just a minute. I picked up this book because I am seeking to make this life better – greater happiness, improved health, better relationships, and greater satisfaction from my work. And you are saying that all of this is an illusion?

Not exactly.

As you will see as you read on, by playing the Game of Awakening we release our attachment to an outcome, and out of this freedom, we may spontaneously manifest those things we desire – because we don't NEED to have them to be happy.

Interestingly, once we realize our happiness is a place we are coming from, not going to, our specific desires for certain things or conditions become preferences, rather than addictions. From the standpoint of this deeper awakening, we recognize that desires, like thoughts and feelings, are waves

The Collective Dark Night of the Soul

that arise and subside in the ocean of awareness, impermanent forms returning to the formless realm from which they arose. In this way, transcendent awareness of who we really are releases attachment to form and outcome – and we are happy to just Be.

Awakening can happen in stages, and it can happen all at once.

As I shared in *For Giving Love*, my awakening was sparked by a spiritual revelation that my mission was to heal with love, and I was fortunate to experience how love heals physical conditions in humans – as well as how it can influence the growth of bacteria, cancer cells, and DNA.

We live in a civilization where the dominant paradigm is that only the material world is "real," and where everything we experience can be explained rationally.

Because of this cultural conditioning, we become attached to the material conditions in our lives and imagine our happiness and wellbeing come from things and conditions outside us. Every time we hear a story or have an experience that cannot be explained by the laws of physical reality as we understand them, the grip of the ordinary world is weakened – and we potentially move closer to awakening to our essential nature.

Forgiveness is an important tool in the Game of

Awakening because it frees us from the prison of the past.

There are many games we can play in life – the money game, the relationship game, the creativity game, the work game – and above and beyond all of these, the Game of Awakening is the Master Game. When we awaken to who we really are, all of the other games are put into perspective.

So...what is this game of awakening, and how do we play?

The Ocean of Awareness & the Game of Awakening

The Game of Awakening is about lifting the veils of the illusion of separation and recognizing wholeness as the inherent reality. There is only One. Not even the appearance of separation can be separate from the One. I could stop here because all else is just Oneness expressing as multiplicity.

There is only One. Not even the appearance of separation can be separate from the One.

One of the simplest yet most profound spiritual metaphors is that of the ocean and the waves as two ways of looking at the One.

The Collective Dark Night of the Soul

As Thich Nhat Hanh said, "If a wave only sees its form, with its beginning and end, it will be afraid of birth and death. But if the wave sees that it is water, identifies itself with the water, then it will be emancipated from birth and death. Each wave is born and is going to die, but the water is free from birth and death."[1]

We're all like waves in the Ocean of Awareness appearing to be separate.

First, there was pure awareness, absolute Source. The wisdom traditions maintain that primordial awareness interacted with itself creating a vibration, the first wave, called Consciousness.

The First Wave – Consciousness

Awareness of Oneness

This First Wave, pure awareness – aware of itself as consciousness – arises and is referred to as "I AM." The "I Am" is also known as "Being," as "I Exist," as "Radical Subject," as "That which looks" – the "I that looks with nothing to look at but itself." When "I Am" looked within as consciousness conscious of itself, it dissolved back into awareness as a wave dissolves in the ocean.

---

[1] Hanh, T. N. (2011). *Awakening of the Heart: Essential Buddhist Sutras and Commentaries.* Parallax Press.

The Second Wave - Duality

The Appearance of Separation

When "I Am" looked out instead of within, and saw "I Am that I Am," this "I Am" consciousness interacted with itself creating the Second Wave, the Thinking Mind. The Thinking Mind divides the whole into self-other, observer-observed, subject-object duality, generating time/space and the multiplicity of forms.

The Third Wave – I/Me/Egoic Mind

The Great Forgetting and the Cause of Suffering

To deepen the mystery, the Thinking Mind somehow folds upon itself and forgets completely that it is consciousness and then behaves as if it's separate from consciousness, forming the Third Wave – the "I/Me/Egoic Self." The Thinking Mind attaches its identity to this egoic self, which then compares and judges itself as "more than" or "less than" other selves, and projects the past into the future, bypassing the present.

The process of forgetting pure awareness is like the moon forgetting that it is reflecting the sun and seeing itself as the source of light.

This sense of separation from consciousness and the focus instead on the ever-changing forms that consciousness takes, is at the core of all fear and suffering, including the fear of death. In my medical practice, I observed that all suffering, distress, and many illnesses derive from this perceived sense of separation.

The Game of Awakening Is the Game of Remembering

The Game of Awakening is the game of remembering the unity of pure awareness, from which everything comes and to which everything returns. Love is the reminder of that unity and the impulse to return to unity. In moving back from Third Wave to Second Wave to First Wave, we dissolve into ever-present Oneness. As we will see later, there are portals to Oneness that allow us to experience this Oneness while still in physical form.

Another way ever-present oneness has been expressed in the Eastern traditions is that form is emptiness and emptiness appears as form since both are composed of the same "substance" – consciousness itself. A classic analogy is that of the sandcastle on the beach that is made of sand temporarily given form. Similarly, consciousness takes shape as form.

And even those forms that appear most unloving and fear-based – war, rejection, resistance, violence, judgment, shame, anger, hatred – are really the one consciousness we call love disguised as separation. To paraphrase The Course In Miracles, all human behavior is either an expression of love or a call for love.

While some would say these behaviors are an expression of our impulse to survive, ultimately none of us survive as a physical form – all the more reason to appreciate the formless, boundless context of loving consciousness. When we release our identification with fear-based separative forms and remember there is only one consciousness assuming many forms, we are home and we are free.

When we release our identification with fear-based separative forms and remember there is only one consciousness assuming many forms, we are home and we are free.

There is a natural relationship between Oneness and love because it is the nature of love to remember and seek unity. When love finds the unity it seeks, all further seeking stops. And when we awaken to the Oneness that is our inherent nature, we realize how much energy we have expended to maintain the illusion of separation. Whenever we feel tossed and thrown by the waves of circumstance and condition, it is helpful to remember the Ocean of Awareness, the ultimate reality.

The Collective Dark Night of the Soul

And yet the illusion of separation is so much a part of our culture, our neurobiology, and such a big part of our self-identity, that we find it hard to imagine who we would be or what we would do without these "precious" wounding stories.

As I have said, in my decades of practice I have found that all suffering, and most illness, can be traced back to this perceived sense of separation. There is a part of ourselves that we find too painful to hold in consciousness. So we separate from it. We disconnect from it, deny it, reject it, repress it, or project it onto others.

Early in our lives or perhaps in our mother's womb, something happened that caused us to feel we're not good enough or not loved, or that our existence is a mistake or a burden. In order to hold ourselves separate from this painful part, we simultaneously separate from others, from the world around us, and most profoundly, from our spiritual essence – from Source.

Now, of course, distinctions are a necessary part of daily life. As we saw earlier in the Ocean of Awareness metaphor, in order for life to exist and reflect upon itself, awareness becomes aware of itself, creating consciousness, the first distinction. Then, consciousness divides itself into subject and object, creating duality, which is just the appearance of separation. Finally, consciousness forgets its Oneness, giving rise to the egoic experience of being a separate self – a stranger in a strange land.

In essence, the Game of Awakening is about forgetting and separating from Oneness and then remembering and returning to ever-present Oneness.

The Game of Awakening is about forgetting and separating from Oneness, and then remembering and returning to ever-present Oneness.

The following diagram shows Pure Awareness's cyclical journey from Oneness and back to Oneness, for the seeming purpose of experiencing duality and playing the Game of Awakening along the way. Through our soul, what we call the Aware Witness, we then dissolve back into the Ocean of Awareness. The Game of Awakening begins and ends with Pure Awareness.

The Collective Dark Night of the Soul

The Game of Awakening

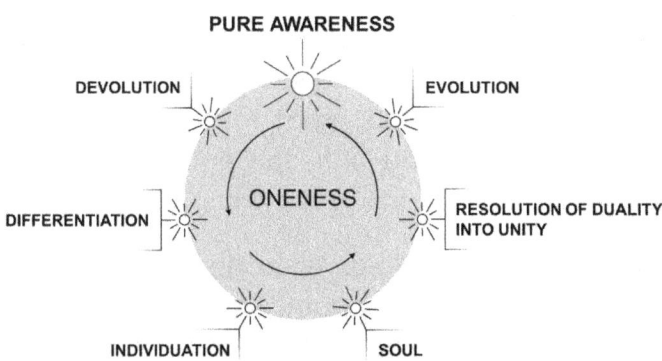

- **ONENESS** BEGINS AND ENDS WITH PURE AWARENESS.

- **Devolution** – Awareness becomes aware of itself creating consciousness.

- **Differentiation** – Consciousness, as part of the outward journey, gives rise to the many forms.

- **Individuation** – Form co-arises and co-exists with consciousness as both form and formless.

- **Soul** – Soul arises and evolves out of consciousness as the increasing simultaneous awareness (the aware witness) of both form and essence as Oneness, thus beginning the inward evolutionary journey home.

- **Resolution of Duality into Unity** – Soul's journey home is aided by resolving the duality of form and essence into unity through love, truth, and will, the portals to Pure Awareness.

- **Evolution** – Soul, entering the portals, dissolves back into pure awareness, completing the Game of Awakening.

Prior to awakening, our tendency is to experience reality as the manifest forms, and not the unmanifest, formless consciousness that gives rise to the forms. In the secular society where only the material world is deemed "real," we are schooled in the differentiation of one form from another.

It's easy for most of us to recognize how we are different from other people and other creatures, and mistake difference for separation. Remembering we are all sourced from the one consciousness appearing as different forms is the spiritual challenge of enlightenment. It is said that the forms are many, the essence is One.

Those initiatory drug experiences in the 1960s and 1970s temporarily liberated many individuals from the cultural filters that reinforced our sep-

The Collective Dark Night of the Soul

aration from life. Experiencing the Holoenergetic® Forgiveness Process, in my book, *For Giving Love,* can fully allow you to remember unity through unconditional love for yourself.

Remembering Unity serves to remind us of what we intrinsically know but have temporarily forgotten. It allows us to reconnect and re-experience those "members" that have been dismembered (separated, cut off) by the limiting sense perceptions, beliefs, and by the veils of our conditioned structures in consciousness.

We are inherently whole. It is only the thinking mind that dismembers us from our essence. It is the thinking mind that divides observer and observed creating subject/object and time/space duality.

It is the "function" of love to make us aware of wholeness – it does not bring us into wholeness because we are already always whole. Through love, we can awaken to Oneness.

And so, Soul, entering the Portals, dissolves back into pure awareness, completing the Game of Awakening.

Chapter 3

Portals to Peace

Peace is a space, not a state. And space doesn't really change, but states do. So if you are in a space that is filled with content, choosing instead to focus on the space (the context) and not the content, can bring you into peace.

What Is Peace?

Peace means no conflict, no disturbance with regard to your thoughts or feelings in the moment, or in your body. You could feel at peace at each of these levels separately or all of them collectively. Then, if there is no disturbance spiritually, meaning if you feel like you are aligned with Source through the aware witness, not conceptually or mentally, but in actual spiritual alignment with source, then you could be in deep abiding alignment with spiritual peace.

When you're feeling this deep peace, you're balanced and aligned physically, emotionally, mentally, and spiritually. There is no disturbance at any of these levels, only stillness, quiet space, calm, and centeredness. And that is a deep peace. That space of peace is ever-present within you, within all of us. You can access that space through the aware witness.

The space of peace is ever-present within you, within all of us.

You can also go directly to it. And this book provides a way to go directly into peace. Regardless of the disturbance, whether pain or illness or any external circumstance, you can go to this place of peace, and just be at peace.

Experiencing the Portals to Peace

What is the access key that opens the portals to peace? It is the shift in focus from content to context – from form to formless – from thinking to being – from form to essence – from the many to the one – from unconscious to conscious – from awareness of content to awareness of awareness. This leads to the evolution of consciousness – which is the game of awakening. The Game of Awakening is the Context.

Anything can be a portal to peace when you become "aware" of it. For example, the part of you that you may be denying or repressing – commonly called the shadow – is most powerful when it rules unconsciously.

Once we become aware of the shadow, when we bring the light of consciousness to bare on the shadow, the shadow as content is transcended by this aware context. We see this in Gestalt Therapy, Voice Dialogue, and Cognitive Therapy, as examples.

Even the command, "Choose Peace Now," shifts the affected person from the content of the conditioned reactivity of the past to the context, the space consciousness of the aware present now. "Choose Peace Now" is a portal to peace.

---

*The command "Choose Peace Now"
is a portal to peace.*

There's a saying, "The wound lets the light in." We refer to that wound as a "treasured wound," because the treasure is the awareness of the wound. The wound is the content. By becoming aware of the wound, you can choose to turn your attention – focused awareness – to what is noticing the awareness. Then dive into this noticer. Dive deeper and deeper until there is no noticer, only awareness itself.

Now the wound has become the treasure. Now you have accessed the divine purpose of being.

Holoenergetic® Portals to Peace

Set aside some quiet and undisturbed times to start experiencing these Holoenergetic® Portals to Peace. For example, in the mornings and/or before sleep.

- Grounding, Aligning, Centering, and the Field of Light
- Conscious Heart Focus
- Balancing Breath
- Accessing Head and Heart Space
- Transpersonal Self Alignment
- Self Harmonization

The *"Conscious Heart Focus"* and *"Balancing Breath"* meditations, narrated by Dr. Laskow, are also available in the *"The Guided Healing Meditations"* MP3 format, on our website store at www.laskow.net.

Note: For the portal processes that are not available on MP3 and narrated by Dr. Laskow – you may find it easier to first record the words in your own voice to playback for your personal use only. Be sure to pause at the right times to allow yourself ample time to experience the process.

PORTAL

Grounding, Aligning, Centering, and the Field of Light

The purpose of this portal is to:

- Bring you into a state of peaceful presence.
- Dissolve duality into unity in your heart.
- Invite higher guidance to be with you.

Follow these simple steps.

Grounding: Begin by taking several slow, deep breaths. Then, as you breathe in, imagine that you are drawing in energy from the core of the earth up through the base of your spine to your heart. As you gently exhale your breath, imagine the energy being released into the center of your chest, into your heart center **grounding** you to the earth.

Aligning: In your relaxed and grounded state, imagine above your head a radiant sun, your transpersonal or soul space. Sense or imagine that you are drawing your next breath in from this radiant sun, down through the top of your head, and release your breath into your heart center. You have now **aligned** with your spiritual nature.

Centering: With your next breath, sense or imagine simultaneously drawing energy up from the core of the earth and down from this radiant sphere through the top of your head. Release your breath into your heart center, fusing the energy coming from above and below — fusing spirit and matter, the masculine and feminine, heaven and earth, **resolving duality into unity in your heart.**

Field of Light: Sense or imagine far above you in inner space a distant star.

And a beam of light descends from this distant star, through the transpersonal space just above your head, through your head, filling your entire body with Divine Light and Love.

Feel this energy radiating beyond your body so that you are now filled, surrounded, guided, and supported by divine light and love.

You have now consciously invited higher guidance to be with you.

PORTAL

Conscious Heart Focus

The purpose of this portal is to:

- Evoke inner peace, centeredness, and expanded awareness.
- Generate harmonious and balanced heart energies.
- Inspire a loving, healing Presence.

This *"Conscious Heart Focus"* meditation, narrated by Dr. Laskow, is also available in the *"The Guided Healing Meditations"* MP3 format, on our website store at www.laskow.net.

You can practice this alone or with a partner, sharing your experiences afterward.

[Preparation]

- Make yourself comfortable, gently close your

Choose Peace Now

eyes, and allow yourself to begin to relax.

- One of the best ways to relax is to become aware of your breathing.

- So just allow yourself now to become aware of your breathing.

- Without efforting just notice that you are breathing in when you are breathing in and that you are breathing out when you are breathing out.

- If other thoughts, feelings, or sensations come to mind, gently but firmly bring your awareness back to your breath.

[Pause]

- Shift attention to the center of your chest, your heart center.

- Slowly breathe in and out as if through the center of your chest for at least three breaths.

- As best you can, recall a wonderful heart-opening experience, and allow yourself to feel these heart-full feelings now – perhaps feelings of love, caring, gratitude, perhaps aliveness, joy, or deep inner peace, flowing in the moment, a sense of oneness or wonderment. Or focus on something that opens your heart, that makes you feel good.

Portals to Peace

- It may be in nature, in solitude, with another, or others.

- Really feel these expansive feelings while continuing to breathe in and out through the center of your chest.

[Pause]

- Become aware of a gift that is gracing your life in this moment – perhaps it's someone or something that you love or care about – perhaps it's simply being alive and aware, here and now, – the gift of life itself – a gift you didn't earn or learn.

  Perhaps it's a love for Source, for that which is beyond understanding, for that which calls you home.

  Allow yourself to feel these heart-felt feelings as you continue to breathe in and out through the center of your chest.

- Now take a deep breath in through the center of your chest, hold it for a moment, and as you release your breath, feel these feelings radiating throughout your entire body. Feel the aliveness, love, caring, joy, gratitude in every atom, every cell of your body. Feel the vibrancy of your inner energy body.

  Simply allow yourself to be in this space.

Conscious Heart Focus
Short Version

Once you feel comfortable with the full Conscious Heart Focus, you can use this short version to move with ease into that peaceful and harmonious state.

- Shift attention to the center of your chest.

- Breath in and out through the center of your chest for at least three breaths.

- Focus on and tune into something that opens your heart and makes you feel good – like switching to a channel that always makes you feel good, that brings a smile to your heart.

PORTAL

Balancing Breath

The purpose of this portal is to:

- Experience aware stillness.
- Invite your intuitive knowing and higher guidance.
- Bring you into balance and heart-brain coherence.

This *"Balancing Breath"* meditation, narrated by Dr. Laskow, is also available in the *"The Guided Healing Meditations"* MP3 format, on our website store at www.laskow.net.

You can practice this alone or with a partner, sharing your experiences afterward.

Choose Peace Now

[Introduction]

Alternate nostril breathing has been practiced for thousands of years in the East. When I was exploring this process in a laboratory hooked up to an electroencephalogram, I noticed that when I picked up one hand to open and close the nostril alternately, it stimulated the contralateral hemisphere of my brain.

So, I decided to simply imagine breath coming in through one nostril and leaving through the other, without my hand, and it produced a kind of balance. I call this the Balancing Breath, which is one of the foundational processes of Holoenergetic® healing.

[Preparation]

- Close your eyes and allow yourself to begin to relax.

- Just becoming aware of your breathing – just aware that when you are breathing in, you are breathing in, and when you are breathing out, you are breathing out.

- And if other thoughts or feelings or sensations arise, just gently but firmly bring your awareness back to your breath.

As you do this exercise, try to involve as many senses as you can. For example, as you breathe in, notice that the air flowing through your nostrils feels cool. Notice how it feels warm in your nostrils as you exhale. As you breathe, air moves the tiny hairs that line your nasal passages. Allow yourself to sense these movements.

Through your breathing, you can consciously influence your body, your feelings, and thoughts, and shift your state of consciousness. The balancing breath links the physical body with soul and spirit, and, in so doing, it allows you to access non-local realms of consciousness.

You will be breathing in through one nostril and out through the other. That is one cycle. You do this for seven cycles. On the next three cycles, you breathe in through both nostrils simultaneously up into the center of your head and release your breath out through the top of your head, following your breath with your mind. So when you release your breath through the top of your head and follow with your mind you may find yourself in an expanded space without boundaries – the space of your aware witness.

[Begin]

Assume a comfortable, relaxed position.

Sense or image breathing in and out as if through the center of your chest.

- Now gently close your eyes and exhale,

allowing your lungs to empty.

- Focus on your left nostril, sense or imagine slowly breathing:
    - in left nostril; out right nostril - one
    - in right; out left - two
    - in left; out right - three
    - in right; out left - four
    - in left; out right - five
    - in right; out left - six
    - in left; out right - seven
    - With the next three breaths, breathe in through both nostrils simultaneously up into the center of your head and release your breath out through the top of your head, following your breath with your mind, opening you to the expanded boundless space of the aware witness.

Continue to breathe in through both nostrils and out through the top of your head.

Listening to the silence...

Notice there is no separation between the silence and the listener.

Portals to Peace

There is no boundary between the silence and the listener of the silence.

There is no inner or outer, no above, no below.

Only aware stillness.

PORTAL

Accessing Head and Heart Space

The purpose of this portal is to:

- Notice foreground and background.
- Notice content and context.
- Notice the difference between head space and heart space.

You can practice this alone or with a partner, sharing your experiences afterward.

Head Space

Imagine your attention inside the back of your head.

- Gently close your eyes and become aware of your breath breathing itself.

Choose Peace Now

- Open your eyes and focus your attention on an object in the room, not a person.

- As you look at the object, see it as if you are seeing it for the first time without thinking about it, naming or labeling it.

- Now, while looking at it pull your attention and your breath inward toward the space inside the back of your head.

- As best you can, notice the space.

- Now, from this space, notice the object.

- The object is in the foreground, the space is the background.

- What do you notice?

Heart Space

Imagine your attention in a space behind your energetically balanced heart and in front of the spine.

- Gently close your eyes and become aware of your breath breathing itself.

- Sense or imagine breathing in and out as if through the center of your chest - your energetic heart, for at least three breaths.

Portals to Peace

- Open your eyes and focus your attention on the same object without thinking about it or naming it.

- Now, while looking at it, pull your attention and breath inward into the space inside the back of your heart. Just have the intention and your awareness will find its way into your heart space.

- As best you can, notice the space.

- Now, from this space, notice the object.

- When you allow yourself to unconditionally, non-judgmentally accept the object exactly as it is, what do you notice?

This space in the head and the heart is the unconditioned space prior to thinking that we all share – a space of unity – a space of truth – a space of love. This is the background context space that never changes – that aspect of the Aware Witness that remains constant regardless of the everchanging foreground perceptions of content, objects and forms.

PORTAL

Transpersonal Self Alignment

The purpose of this portal is to:

- Experience generating conscious heart energies.
- Send yourself loving, healing energy beyond space and time.
- Establish alignment with your soul and spirit.
- Help you open to more love, peace, and compassion for yourself.
- Open to your own inner wisdom.

You can practice this alone or with a partner, sharing your experiences afterward.

[Preparation]

- Gently close your eyes and allow yourself to begin to relax.

Choose Peace Now

[Conscious Heart Focus]

- Breathe in and out as if through the center of your chest, your energetic heart center. If other thoughts come to mind, gently but firmly bring your awareness back to your breath. Slowly breathe in and out through your heart center for at least three breaths.

    o As best you can, focus on a wonderful heart-opening experience, something that always makes you feel good, and allow yourself to feel these heart-felt feelings now – perhaps feelings of love, caring, gratitude, perhaps aliveness, joy, or deep inner peace, flowing in the moment, a sense of oneness. Allow yourself to feel these expansive feelings while continuing to breathe in and out through the center of your chest.

    o Now take a deep breath in through the center of your chest, hold it for a moment, and as you release your breath, feel these feelings radiating throughout your entire body.

    o Feel the aliveness, love, caring, joy, gratitude in every atom, every cell of your body.

    o Feel the vibrancy of your inner energy body.

Portals to Peace

[Image]

- Now, sense or imagine yourself sitting in a chair in front of you, facing you.

[Heart Link]

- With your eyes still closed, focus your attention on the heart center of your own image sitting before you now and sense or imagine a beam of light extending from your heart center to your self image's heart center linking you heart to heart.

[Transpersonal Link]

- Now sense or imagine, just above your head a radiant sun – your transpersonal or soul space and sense or imagine a beam of light extending from your radiant sun to your image's sun, linking you soul to soul, and a beam of light descending from the sun of your image through the top of its head to its heart.

- Sense or imagine, extending from your shoulder blades translucent iridescent wings of light. Gently, lovingly embrace your self image in wings of light.

[Pause]

- Aware of your heart-to-heart link, allow yourself to feel these heartfelt feelings for the one who sits before you now, beyond the conditioned personality, physicality, and form with no judgment or comparison, without condition, reason, or cause.

- Feel an unconditional acceptance for this being exactly as this being is in this moment.

[Feel these feelings]

- Allow yourself to feel these heart-felt feelings for its soul and spirit embodied in form that expresses both uniqueness and unity, as you continue to breathe in and out through the center of your chest.

[Deep Breath]

- Draw a deep breath in through the center of your chest and HOLD it.

[Release]

- As the energy reaches its peak, release your feeling-filled breath from your heart to your image's heart through the connecting beam of light.

[Sense]

- Sense or imagine its body and energy field becoming radiant with loving light.

[Be]

- Now, release all effort and intention and just BE.

[Pause]

- Silently thank the image of yourself for receiving your love. Now, sense or imagine your image standing up, coming to you, turning around, sitting down in your lap, merging with you, and becoming one. Allow yourself to feel this now.

- There is only One appearing as many, revealing itself as love.

- Allow yourself to feel the One Love.

- When you're ready, gently open your eyes, alive and aware, here now.

PORTAL

Self Harmonization Process

The purpose of this portal is to:

- Learn to love yourself.
- Heal into wholeness.
- Function through the aware witness.

You can practice this alone or with a partner, sharing your experiences afterward.

[Preparation]

- Close your eyes, allow yourself to relax.

- Become aware of the flow of your breath.

- Ground, align, center.

- Field of light: filled, surrounded, guided, and supported.

Choose Peace Now

- Take yourself to the most serene, peaceful place or space you know or can imagine.

Observer/Witness Exercise in Awareness

- Let the image and thought, and fragrance of a red rose arise in your awareness. Now let the image and thought of the rose dissolve back into awareness.

  Thank you.

- Let an expansive emotion or feeling arise into your awareness. Now let the emotion dissolve back into your awareness.

  Thank you.

- Let a contractive emotion or feeling arise into your awareness. Now let the emotion dissolve back into your awareness.

  Thank you.

- Let a sensation you are presently feeling in your body arise into your awareness with your next breath – the sensation of your lungs being filled with air. (Or feel your bottom on the chair.) Now let that sensation dissolve back into awareness.

  Thank you.

Portals to Peace

- Let a belief about yourself arise into your awareness.

Thank you.

- Now let that belief dissolve back into awareness.

Thank you.

- Let the image of yourself (as if looking into mirror) arise into your awareness and think of your name. Now let the image and name dissolve back into awareness.

Thank you.

- Let the idea of who you are come to mind. Now let the idea dissolve into awareness.

Thank you.

- Let the thought, "What will the next thought be?" arise in awareness.

Thank you.

- Notice the next phenomenon that arises in awareness. Now let it dissolve back into awareness.

Thank you.

[Self Harmonization]

- As this observing awareness, notice the stillness, the peace in this space, free of identification with thoughts, feelings, sensations. Aware of the thoughts, feelings, sensations, and experiences arising, existing, and disappearing like bubbles in the ocean of awareness – totally free – boundless, infinite – pure awareness.

[Pause]

- As the witnessing eye of pure awareness, become aware once again of thoughts, feelings, and body sensations as they come and go.

- Allow whatever arises to arise, whatever subsides to subside.

[Phase Shift]

- Now, as the aware witness, allow a stressful or unresolved issue from your past to come to mind.

[Pause]

Portals to Peace

- Be aware of your mind experiencing the issue (give yourself time to contemplate each one):
    - as story
    - as thoughts
    - as memories
    - as feelings
    - as sensations
    - as images
    - as choices
    - as decisions
    - as beliefs...
- Just notice these experiences as they come and go in awareness.
- From this observing awareness, what is the lesson being learned?

[Pause]

- Now as the aware witness with its infinite wisdom and love:
    - compassionately release what needs to be released,
    - forgive what needs to be forgiven,

Choose Peace Now

- heal what needs to be healed,
- love what needs to be loved,
- bring all into wholeness so that our form and Essence are One.

[Phase Shift]

- Now once again, through the eye of the aware witness, view this body-mind phenomenon, with its sensations, thoughts, feelings, images, and ideas. Feel the boundless infinite love that arises in awareness for that part of yourself manifesting as physical form, substance, and energy.

- Know that healing into wholeness has occurred.

- Take a deep breath and gently open your eyes.

Chapter 4

The Collective Dawn of the Soul

It is the destiny of form to return to its underlying unity – its source. And love is the reminder, the unifying force.

Soul is the interface between personal form (personality) and spiritual nature.

At Home in Peace

The Collective Dawn of the Soul is Peace. When we wake up to who we really are, this is unity, this is Oneness.

Dawn is the first light. This is the light of the soul. The light of consciousness, the first wave, which comes from the awareness of awareness.

And it is also the delight of the soul! It is waking up from the collective darkness, the dark night of the soul, the apparent chaos that is a prelude to transformation, to a new order, and a higher level of human consciousness.

This awareness can empower us to live our purpose more intentionally.

Thirst for Life

What is thirst? It is a seeking to be fulfilled, satisfied. It is a desire, a need, a want, depending on how it is perceived. What is life? Life has an inherent impulse to become conscious of itself. A place where stillness and movement overlap and co-exist. A movement. Existence has an inherent impulse, then, to flow to the ocean. So, life is about flow. And what flows? The answer is consciousness flows.

When do you feel most alive? You feel most alive when you are fully present and in the flow. Nisargadatta Maharaj, the Hindu sage, said, "Wisdom is knowing I am nothing, love is knowing I am everything, and between the two my life flows." Life is a river current of ever-changing forms returning to the ocean of primordial consciousness.

Life flows between the unmanifest and the manifest, between nothing and everything, between essence and form, between unity and duality; and truth is being fully present to what is.

So, what quenches the thirst for life? Is it the water? What is the water? The magical elixir that satisfies, fulfills, and completes us. Is it fame and

The Collective Dawn of the Soul

fortune with its ups and downs? Is it the agony and ecstasy of relationship with its challenges? No. It is coming home to your true nature. Consciousness itself, embracing the coexisting flow of form and essence, stillness speaking, emptiness dancing, coming home to oneness. You're in the flow of life.

You're fully alive when you are present to the truth of what is, what is happening in the moment. Being conscious of consciousness, not operating from past conditioning or future projections. Loving and accepting yourself exactly as you are.

I have found that in addition to being fully present, one of the best ways to be fully in the flow, to flow with the current of life, is to unconditionally love yourself exactly as you are, which is the truth of what is so right now. Why is that?

Love seeks unity just as knowing seeks truth. All seeking is a desire, a movement toward the object of desire, or if an aversion, a movement away from; therefore, all seeking, all desire, is movement.

I have found that in addition to being fully present, one of the best ways to be fully in the flow, to flow with the current of life, is to unconditionally love yourself exactly as you are, which is the truth of what is so right now.

When love merges with the unity it seeks, all movement, all seeking ceases, and what remains is stillness. Similarly, when knowing finds the truth that it's seeking, all movement toward the truth stops. What remains is stillness, so both love and truth lead to stillness. This stillness is beyond description but reported as an experience. It's also called freedom, or peace beyond understanding, joy, emptiness, nothing, oneness, unity, source, opening, totality, God, primordial consciousness.

Come home to your essential nature and the thirst for life will be totally satisfied. All that is left is to flow, to be the ever-changing, never changing, co-existing flow of life, what comes and what goes. Unattached to the outcome, and at peace.

Your Life Purpose: Ways to Express Your Essential Nature

What is it that really brought you here into this life? What do you really, really want? What is the life purpose that brought you here?

Well, let's look at a list of Holoenergetic® Life Purposes, and see what one or more purposes you pick from the list.

The Collective Dawn of the Soul

Holoenergetic® Life Purposes

- To learn that you consciously create your experience of reality.

- To learn to have fun, to be happy, to enjoy and to experience the bliss of being.

- To unfold and deepen communion with your Essential Nature – that which is most representative of oneness.

- To experience and express love – its unity and uniqueness (you are One and one of a kind).

- To discover your own unique qualities and talents.

- To be of service through spiritual guidance.

- To learn how to heal into wholeness.

One life purpose is to learn that you consciously create your experience of reality. Another one is to learn to have fun, to be happy, to enjoy, and experience the bliss of being.

Another purpose may be to unfold and deepen your communion with your Essential Nature. Another is to experience and express love, both its unity and uniqueness, embracing the duality within the unity. Another is to discover your own unique qualities and talents. Another is to be of service to others through spiritual guidance. And, another is to learn to heal into wholeness.

Is there some other loving life purpose that energizes you?

Ways Essence Expresses Itself Through You

This diagram shows ways that essence expresses itself through you.

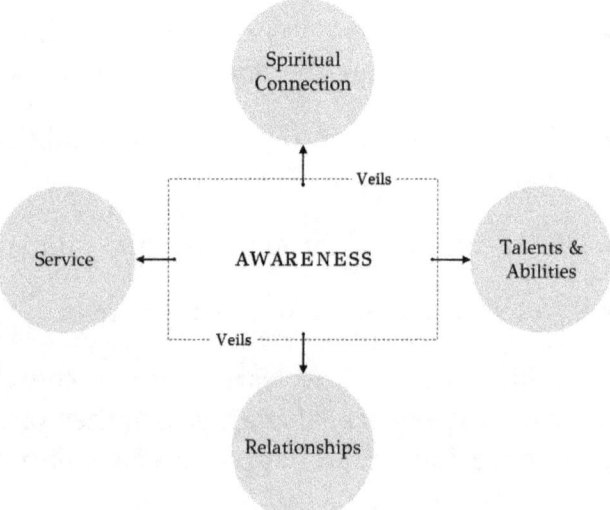

In the center, that's consciousness itself – Pure Awareness. The box around the light of consciousness represents the veils that obscure Pure Awareness. Then there are places where these arrows pierce the veils, which include our spiritual connection, talents and abilities, relationships, and

The Collective Dawn of the Soul

our service. And to be of service to others through spiritual guidance. The talents and abilities that are unique are not necessarily in service to others, but they are an expression of the divine.

In other words, somebody like Mozart or Beethoven may not have been what you would normally call a spiritual being, but they were inspired by Spirit, by Source. I'm mentioning them because they are well known as geniuses. So, each one of us also has our own unique qualities and talents, inspired by Source, by Spirit. And, then specifically to be in service of others. That's another way that our inner light can shine forth through these veils. And, then to learn to heal into wholeness and to directly align with wholeness, with Source, with Spirit.

So what are the life purposes that you bring? And, you can have a number of them. It's good to make them conscious. It's interesting that one of the life purposes is to learn to have fun, to learn to be happy, to learn to enjoy and to experience the bliss of being.

Some people are fortunate in just being happy. Others must learn. And, what is happiness to you? Is it fulfilling perceived needs or wants? If you could have all that you want, would that bring you happiness? There is confusion in some people about what is pleasure and what is happiness. Pleasure is limited.

Happiness doesn't come from outside. Happiness comes from inside. It has to do with the sense of fulfillment, joy, and being at peace.

The Intuitive Co-Creator Process

When we have a sense of our life purpose or purposes, the Intuitive Co-Creator Process is a powerful tool to align our intention and will with Source so that our heart's desire can become our focused intention, and therefore manifest. The Intuitive Co-Creator helps us focus the energy liberated through this process to give us more joy, peace, and freedom.

Purpose: Learning to co-create your reality and manifest what you want. This can be life purpose, a specific event, a state of body and mind or even an expanded consciousness.

You can also get a recording of this process, which is included in *"Guided Healing Meditations"* on my website: www.laskow.net.

Establish a Timeframe

Before you begin this process, take some time to decide on a timeframe for manifesting what you want. It's important to set a date to aim for. Perhaps it will be by your birthday, holiday, special event, or any date that feels right for you.

The Collective Dawn of the Soul

Optional: Start with Grounding, Aligning, and Centering.

Recognize

Is there something you truly want with all your heart? If so, silently state it now and allow yourself to sense how you would feel when it manifests. Take as much time as you need.

Where are these feelings located in your body? Do you feel it in your heart? Do you want it with all your heart in this moment? [If "yes" bypass option.]

[Option:] If not, allow yourself to sense from where the desire for this manifestation originates and what is really wanted. Then reconsider what you want to manifest. Unless you want it with all your heart this process will not work as efficiently.

If you truly want this with all your heart right now, silently choose and intend that this or better manifest in your life within a specific time frame.

Take whatever time you need.

Now, disengage the mind's attention – tell the mind to stop for a moment, to suspend all thoughts, images, feelings, or sensations associated with this manifestation.

Resonate

Shift attention to your heart area. Slowly and

deeply breathe in and out as if through the center of your chest for at least three breaths. Allow yourself to release all effort now and just relax – relax while breathing in and out as if through the center of your chest.

Recall a time when you felt really good, a time when you had a heart-opening experience. Focus on it, and allow yourself to feel these feelings now – perhaps feelings of love, laughter, joy, inner peace, harmony – flowing in the moment. As best you can, really feel these expansive feelings while continuing to breathe in and out through your heart center.

Release

Focusing all your awareness within your heart, bring what you want into your heart, and ask your heart's intuitive wisdom, intelligence and love to manifest this in the most beneficial and effective way for your highest good within the specific time frame.

When you are ready, draw a deep breath into your heart, and as you release your breath, entrust your heart's desire to the universe.

Reform

Now allow your heart's intention to synchronistically organize the universal field of all possibilities to manifest this desired outcome.

Imagine and picture the successful outcome in

The Collective Dawn of the Soul

your mind and feel it in your heart. Feel the gratitude in your heart in advance of the actual outcome. Feel as if it has already happened.

Finally, intend to take any action needed to bring the manifestation into being and determine the first step.

Know that manifestation has begun.

Epilogue

Love is the Way

There is only one appearing as many, revealing itself as Love.

Love is the universal harmonic that, through resonance of relatedness, brings us into unity.

Love Is Unity

In my book, *For Giving Love*, I talk about love as the impulse toward unity. Whatever we feel love for, we want to merge with and become resonantly one with. And ultimately, we want to become one with the Divine.

As a concept, the word love refers to two principles: the Relativity Principle of conditioned love, and the Unity Principle of non-conditioned love.

The Relativity Principle

The Relativity Principle suggests that at the level of duality, everything is related to and connected to everything else. And love is the connection. Love is the link within duality. Love links duality to duality. This is "horizontal" love, and it refers to conditioned love.

Horizontal love: Most of the time, when we talk about love, we are talking about relatedness. We want to connect with, merge with another individual, beloved place, or activity. Horizontal love is conditioned love in that it depends on connection with some "other" within duality.

As part of our human experience, there is nothing wrong with "horizontal" love within duality, directed toward other people, places, and things. However, the boundless peace that comes from "vertical" love, like the sun, shines equally on all.

The Unity Principle

The Unity Principle suggests that there is only one appearing as many, revealing itself as love. Love links duality to unity, embracing everything and nothing, the form and formless as one. This is "vertical" love.

Vertical love: This is the non-conditioned love that extends from duality to Unity, that aligns matter with Spirit, form with essence – spontaneously taking us beyond the relatedness of duality into oneness.

Epilogue

Beyond pain or pleasure, beyond joy or sadness, the context of non-conditioned love opens us to boundless freedom and peace.

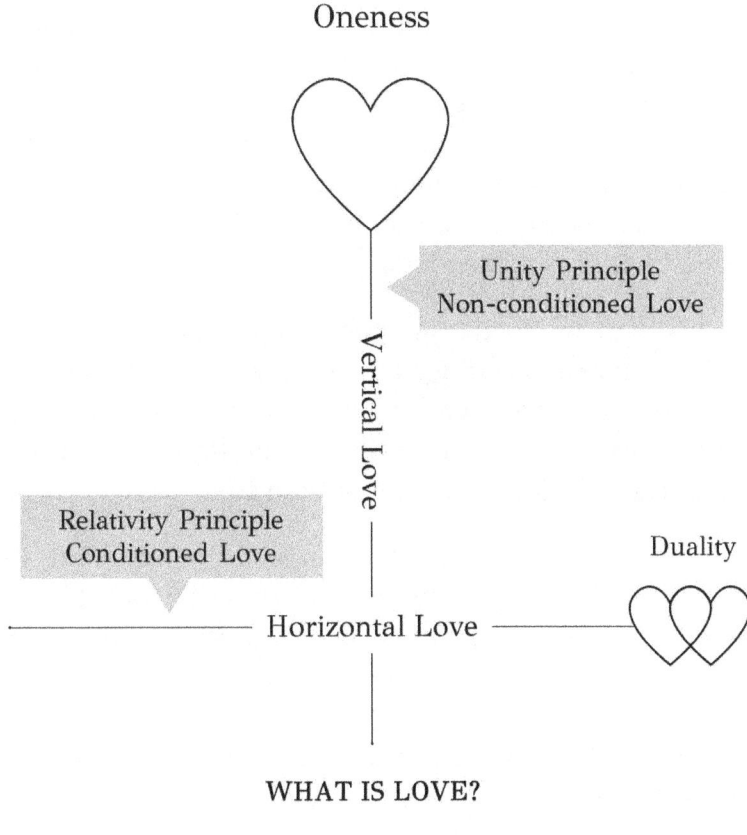

WHAT IS LOVE?

Beyond pain or pleasure, beyond joy or sadness, the context of non-conditioned love opens us to boundless freedom and peace.

Choose Peace Now

Sometimes we say love is ever-present like the sun, but the sun actually has a limited existence; so we can say that love is ever-present like space. However, we don't recognize the space because our nervous systems are not designed to recognize space, the formless nature of our being. Instead, our nervous system is designed to focus on the content, what is contained within the space, the space which is defined as the distance between two objects. Our nervous system is not activated by space, but rather by forms and possessions.

When we focus on space, that is peace! Because when there is nothing, no thing, we feel stillness, we feel peace. There could even be flow, the flow of consciousness. It is the peace of the flow of life itself. Beyond words, beyond understanding.

Even Stephen Hawking has expressed that we don't really know how the universe began. This is an example of beyond understanding. In other words, at the most fundamental level, the very origin of our universe is beyond understanding. We don't understand how we got here, and how the universe was created.

So given that, can you just relax into that space of being beyond understanding? Knowing that life itself is what is in the space of the moment. Asking why is just a mental question for which there is no answer. And, if you accept that, then there's a surrender to, an acceptance of the space beyond

Epilogue

knowing, beyond understanding. When you accept this, you are choosing peace now. You are experiencing the light of consciousness.

When we transcend from conditioned to non-conditioned love, from duality into unity, that is where we will find peace. We don't need to understand unity. We only need to know how to access it.

When we transcend from conditioned to non-conditioned love, from duality into unity, that is where we will find peace beyond the understanding of the mind.

In the Game of Awakening, when awareness becomes aware of itself, that creates a consciousness which is your essential nature. It is consciousness aware of awareness. But if you go back even further, there is Pure Awareness, that oneness beyond the form, which is your **true** nature.

Choose Peace Now – Just BE.

Afterword

Ode to Mind

Love is an awakening to Oneness at the deepest level, an acknowledgment of the unity of every thing.

There are gurus in India who have said that it is important to kill the mind, to destroy the ego. However, I have continued to feel that this is not unity, that this does not represent non-conditioned love. Rather, I feel it is more about embracing and transcending the mind, but not killing it.

And so, one night, while at an ashram in India, I was spontaneously inspired to write the following letter:

Several nights ago upon retiring I called upon my spiritual guides to be with me and then I entrusted myself to my Self.

In the middle of the night, I awakened overwhelmed with such love and compassion.

Afterword

Through tears, I wrote what follows.

All distinctions between mind and self are notions. All is One and love relates All to the One. Love is All.

I, the mind, now have such trust in you, my Self, I melt into your bosom like a baby at its mother's breast.

I, your Self, hold you, dear mind, to my breast with such tender love – for I am your source and you are my child.

This baby, this mind, this body, did not know it was a child of the Self. It thought it was alone. It was scared – born so vulnerable and dependent, exposed to events beyond its comprehension, conditioned by its experiences and environment – it thought it was alone.

This produced such suffering, such pain, such suffering and pain. It came into being to make distinctions of form and substance within the Oneness and got lost in the separations of its own making, creating subject/object, self/non-self and believing them to be real.

Such suffering and pain when it forgot its source, its Self, and turned outward in a desperate attempt to survive on its own not knowing it was pursuing an illusion – a phantom of its own

Epilogue

creation.

It did not know it was lost. All it wanted was love. All it wanted was to once again be part of the Self.

Come home to me, dear one. Let me hold you and love you. You are born, nurtured and you peacefully die in my emptiness One with All.

Your own Self,
Shankar
aka Leonard Laskow

What Is Holoenergetic® Healing?

The Holoenergetic® model allows us to go beyond symptom relief and connect to the original source of separation. Often related to an earlier experience of stress that our brain has interpreted in terms of survival to help us overcome the experience, eventually, it leads us to feel the separation from our authentic, deep nature.

Holoenergetic® healing tools offer us a way to identify and understand these limited patterns and beliefs, to free ourselves from them, and to replace them with feelings of security, fullness, and love that celebrate life.

Holoenergetic® healing tools are based on the awareness that, as we move toward wholeness through love, the enormous amount of energy we use to maintain the illusion of separation from Unity is released and can be directed towards healing the body, resolving emotional conflicts, improving creativity, and supporting personal transformation.

www.Laskow.net

About Leonard Laskow, M.D.

Leonard Laskow, M.D. is a Stanford-trained Life Fellow of the American College of Obstetrics and Gynecology, former Chief of OB-GYN at the Community Hospital of the Monterey Peninsula in Carmel, California, and has served as faculty at the University of California, San Francisco.

He was a founding diplomate of the American Board of Integrative Holistic Medicine and a former member of Heartmath Institute's Scientific Advisory Board. He served as a US Naval Flight Surgeon in Vietnam.

Dr. Laskow has done seminal research with biophysicists, neurochemists and crystallographers on the impact of information and coherent energy on cancer cells, DNA, the growth of bacteria, and water.

He coined the term Holoenergetic® Healing, by which he means healing with the energy of the "whole." The principles of Holoenergetic® Healing are presented in Dr. Laskow's breakthrough book, *Healing with Love*.

Dr. Laskow has written three books and taught internationally at medical centers, universities, and holistic institutes and worked as an consultant in Behavioral and Energie Medicine for over 35 years. Today he is retired and lives in Switzerland.

www.Laskow.net

About Maddisen K. Krown, Ph.D.

Maddisen K. Krown, PhD, is a Professional Coach and Conscious Leadership Consultant who guides her clients in living vital lives of purpose, awareness, compassion, and fulfillment.

In 2007, after being introduced to Dr. Leonard Laskow and his breakthrough book, *Healing with Love*, Maddisen worked with him as a client. Her experiences with Holoenergetic® Healing were profound, thus inspiring Maddisen to train with Dr. Laskow as a Holoenergetic® Practitioner. She continues to practice Holoenergetic® Healing with her private clients.

Maddisen also enjoys her role as Executive Coach at BetterManager, an international leadership development firm whose mission is to make thriving at work the norm.

She is a featured author in the book, *Success In Any Season: Inspiring Stories of Power and Healing*. And currently resides on the East Coast in the U.S.

Working with Dr. Leonard Laskow and Sama Schurter Laskow on his third book, *Choose Peace Now*, has been a blessing and great honor for her.

www.MaddisenKrown.com

Also by Leonard Laskow, M.D.

Healing with Love: A Breakthrough Mind/Body Medical Program For Healing Yourself And Others

For Giving Love: Awakening Your Essential Nature Through Love and Forgiveness

Available at www.Laskow.net
and www.Amazon.com

About Green Heart Living Press

Green Heart Living Press publishes inspirational books and stories of transformation, making the world a more loving and peaceful place, one book at a time.

You can meet Green Heart authors on the Green Heart Living YouTube channel and the Green Heart Living Podcast.

www.GreenHeartLiving.com

www.ingramcontent.com/pod-product-compliance
Lightning Source LLC
Chambersburg PA
CBHW032249080426
42735CB00008B/1066